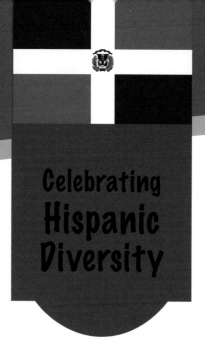

Celebrating
Hispanic
Diversity

THE PEOPLE
AND CULTURE OF THE
DOMINICAN
REPUBLIC

Ian Emminizer

PowerKiDS
press™

New York

Published in 2018 by The Rosen Publishing Group, Inc.
29 East 21st Street, New York, NY 10010

First Edition

Editor: Theresa Morlock
Book Design: Rachel Rising

Photo Credits:Cover KIKE CALVO/VWPICS/Alamy Stock Photo; Cover (background) Buena Vista Images/Photodisc/Getty Images; Cover, p. 1 https://commons.wikimedia.org/wiki/File:Flag_of_the_ Dominican_Republic.svg; p. 5 photopixel/Shutterstock.com; p. 6 Seaphotoart/Shutterstock.com; pp. 7, 19 Reinhard Dirscherl/Corbis Documentary/Getty Images; p. 9 https://commons.wikimedia.org/w/index. php?title=File:Caritas_Enriquillo.jpg&oldid=209012695; p. 11 GiuseppeCrimeni/Shutterstock.com; p. 13 Zoran Karapancev/Shutterstock.com; p.15 David Pou/Shutterstock.com; p. 17 Lapina/Shutterstock.com; p. 21 Alex Wong/Getty Images News/Getty Images; p. 23 Jane Sweeney/AWL Images/Getty Images; p. 25 Salim October/Shutterstock.com; p. 27 George Gojkovich/Getty Images Sport/Getty Images; p. 29 a katz/Shutterstock.com; p. 30 Brothers Good/Shutterstock.com.

Cataloging-in-Publication Data

Names: Emminizer, Ian.
Title: The people and culture of the Dominican Republic / Ian Emminizer.
Description: New York : PowerKids Press, 2018. | Series: Celebrating Hispanic diversity | Includes index.
Identifiers: ISBN 9781538327043 (pbk.) | ISBN 9781508163084 (library bound) | ISBN 9781538327487 (6 pack)
Subjects: LCSH: Dominican Republic–Juvenile literature.
Classification: LCC F1934.2 E46 2018 | DDC 972.93–dc23

Manufactured in the United States of America

CPSIA Compliance Information: Batch #BW18PK: For Further Information contact Rosen Publishing, New York, New York at 1-800-237-9932

CONTENTS

WELCOME TO THE DOMINICAN REPUBLIC!

The Dominican Republic is a Caribbean nation that shares the island of Hispaniola with Haiti. It's approximately 237 miles (381 km) west of Puerto Rico and 600 miles (966 km) southeast of the United States. The nation's lively **customs** and history, as well as the natural beauty of the island, all contribute to a fascinating culture.

Many different peoples have ruled the island throughout its history. The first inhabitants came on canoes from South America to enjoy the island's natural bounty. When Christopher Columbus landed there in 1492, he also recognized the island's value and established a Spanish colony. Before Dominican independence, control of the nation passed back and forth between Spain, France, and Haiti. The culture and **ancestry** of today's Dominicans come from many different **traditions** and backgrounds. **Indigenous** groups, Europeans, and Africans have all become part of the Dominican story.

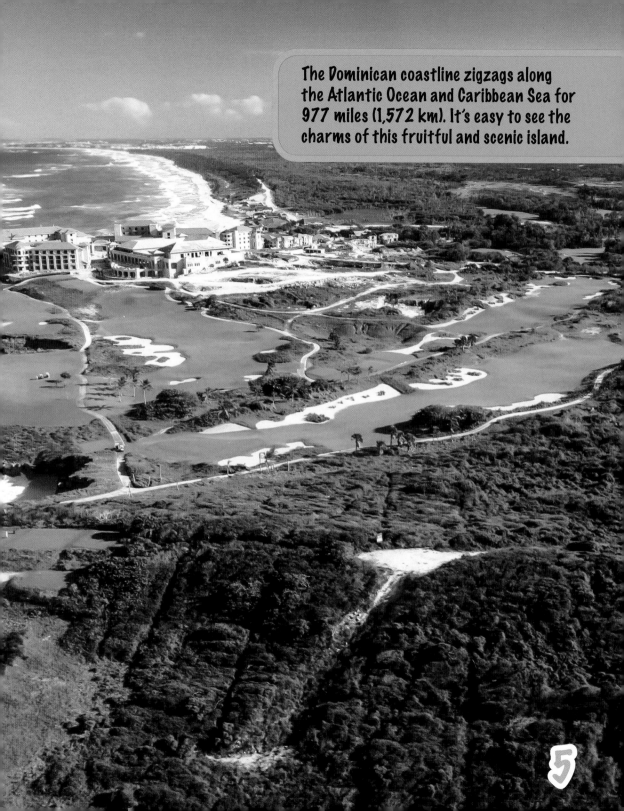

The Dominican coastline zigzags along the Atlantic Ocean and Caribbean Sea for 977 miles (1,572 km). It's easy to see the charms of this fruitful and scenic island.

A TROPICAL PARADISE

The Dominican Republic is located on the island of Hispaniola. It is the second-largest island in the Caribbean. The Dominican Republic takes up the island's eastern side, with Haiti to the west. Hispaniola is divided by five mountain ranges and is home to the Caribbean's highest point, Pico Duarte, and lowest point, Lago Enriquillo. The climate is generally comfortable. However, hurricanes often hit the area and can be very destructive. They may result in the death of many people.

The Dominican Republic is known for white, sandy beaches and rich marine life. Manatees, dolphins, and humpback whales are common. You can spot sea turtles, tropical fish, and corals while snorkeling!

The landscape of the Dominican Republic is marked by different climates, plants, and animals. Mahogany, ebony, and juniper trees grow in lush rain forests. Animals include parrots, snakes, iguanas, and solenodons. The solenodon is one of only two surviving mammals native to the island. A ratlike creature, it kills prey with its poisonous bite.

INDIGENOUS ANCESTORS

The Taíno people lived on Hispaniola when Europeans arrived in 1492. The first Taínos were probably Arawak Indians from the Amazon, who settled on the island around 400 BC. A peaceful people, they divided Hispaniola into five sections, each ruled by a chief. The Taíno people were skilled at farming and fishing. They created cave paintings, pottery, and woven materials. They also played a ball game called *batu* that served as a way to settle disagreements. The words "hurricane," "barbecue," "canoe," and "hammock" come from the Taíno language.

Under European rule, the Taíno population quickly decreased because of sickness, violence, slavery, and starvation. The remaining Taínos were forced to accept Spanish culture. Elements of the Taíno lifestyle still survive, and 15 to 18 percent of Dominicans have Taíno ancestry.

These Taíno stone carvings are called Las Caritas, or the Little Faces. They can be found near Lago Enriquillo in caves that may have sheltered the earliest inhabitants of Hispaniola.

African Slave Trade

As the Taíno people nearly died out, the Spanish looked to Africa for a source of slave labor. Over half a million West Africans were forced onto slave ships bound for Hispaniola beginning in 1520. If they survived the journey, they were put to work in the mines and sugar cane fields that made Hispaniola a wealthy colony. Slavery was outlawed in 1822, when Haiti briefly united Hispaniola. Most of today's Dominicans have a mixture of African and European ancestry.

HISTORICAL FIGURES

After the Taínos, the island of Hispaniola was ruled by other countries. Juan Pablo Duarte is considered the father of the Dominican Republic. He led an effort to claim independence from Haiti in 1843, then fled the country after that effort failed. Thanks to Duarte's followers, the country achieved freedom in 1844 and was renamed after the main city of Santo Domingo. Duarte returned, but he was soon **exiled** by his opponents. Nevertheless, his role in the liberation of the country is still celebrated.

The Dominican Republic has a violent and troubled history. It was run by wealthy landowners for decades and was often under the power of **dictators**. A major democratic election was not held until 1962, when Juan Bosch became president. Bosch, who was both a poet and a politician, was overthrown less than a year later by the military. He is remembered for his literary achievements and honesty.

Juan Pablo Duarte is buried at Altar de la Patria, or Altar of the Homeland, in Santo Domingo.

The Mirabal Sisters

The Mirabal sisters, also known as "las Mariposas" (the butterflies), organized a movement against dictator Rafael Trujillo in 1959. As a result, three of the four sisters were murdered. Their story inspired others to defeat Trujillo and establish a democracy in the Dominican Republic. Today, the sisters are remembered as heroes. Some of their children carry on their legacy as politicians and spokespeople for justice and equality.

RELIGION AND BELIEFS

Christopher Columbus and Spanish missionaries first brought the ideas and customs of Catholicism to the Dominican Republic. Today, most Dominicans are Roman Catholic. However, many people identify as Catholic without necessarily practicing the religion.

The combining of Catholicism with folk traditions or other religions is common. Some Dominicans hold festivals to celebrate *fiestas patronales*, which are feast days held to celebrate a city or town's patron saint. Patron saints are religious figures believed to offer protection and guidance. *Fiestas patronales* are celebrated with music, prayers, and food.

Nuestra Señora de la Altagracia, the Virgin of the Highest Grace, is the most important religious figure in the Dominican Republic. She is the country's official patron saint.

The Cathedral of Saint Mary of the Incarnation in Santo Domingo is the oldest cathedral in the Americas. In the early 1500s, builders spent three decades working to create this impressive Catholic church.

13

CELEBRATIONS

Festivals and holidays make for lively events in the Dominican Republic. Every Sunday in February, Dominicans celebrate Carnival with parades, **elaborate** costumes, music, and dancing. The country has been observing the holiday since 1510!

Dominican roots are highlighted during this exciting time as Taíno, African, and European traditions come together. Cities throughout the Dominican Republic hold special events, but one of the largest occurs on the last Sunday of February in the town of La Vega. It's even more festive because it falls so close to Dominican Independence Day on February 27.

Catholic holidays are also important in the Dominican Republic. They include the special days celebrating saints, Christmas traditions, and the celebration of Semana Santa, or Holy Week. Originally, Carnival was celebrated just before Semana Santa.

Many Dominicans wear colorful masks and costumes during Carnival. Some characters, such as the Diablos Cojuelos, appear every year. These demons dance through the events trying to frighten people!

FRESH AND DELICIOUS!

Meals are a very social and important part of life in the Dominican Republic. The largest meal at midday is a time to relax and share food with friends or family. Cooking in the Dominican Republic is influenced by Spanish, African, and Taíno food; as a whole, it's called *comida criolla*. This is common Caribbean cuisine.

Dominican recipes make use of the many wonderful foods available on the island. Coastal areas enjoy plentiful seafood, such as fish, conch, crab, octopus, and shrimp. Bananas and plantains are especially popular and are often cooked, mashed, and mixed with other foods. Other common ingredients include rice, potatoes, yucca, cassava, and goat meat.

One classic Dominican dish is called *la bandera*, or the flag, because the colors of the dish reflect the country's flag. It is made with white rice, red beans, meat, salad, and green plantains.

Tropical fruits flourish on the island and provide a good source of nutrition for Dominicans. Mangos, bananas, papayas, passion fruit, coconuts, guavas, pineapples, and melons are grown across the country.

Taíno Bread

The recipe for *casabe*, a flatbread made from cassava or yucca, was inherited from the Taíno people. Cassava is a vegetable that grows easily and quickly in the Caribbean. Its roots are gathered, peeled, soaked, ground, pressed, and then molded into round shapes. The Taíno cooked *casabe* over open fires, but most modern Dominicans use a griddle. The traditional bread can be dressed up with butter, garlic, or vegetables. It's often eaten with soup, stew, and traditional meals.

ART OF THE ISLAND

The earliest art in the Dominican Republic can be viewed in many of the island's natural caves, where Taíno people recorded their stories and beliefs. The carvings and drawings they left behind offer a glimpse into their interesting lives and creative power. Many of these charcoal drawings are realistic and show how their makers looked at nature. Others are imaginative, combining animal and human figures in magical ways.

Modern art in the Dominican Republic is displayed in museums, galleries, and other public places. Many amateur artists sell their colorful paintings on the streets. Santo Domingo and the town of Altos de Chavón are filled with the studios of Dominican and international artists. The work of popular artists often illustrates and **interprets** life in the Dominican Republic.

Humans and animals interact in this cave drawing from La Linea Limestone Cave. It's located in Los Haitises National Park. What can you see?

19

WRITERS AND BOOKS

Although the Taíno **expressed** themselves through art and storytelling, they had no written language. Some of the first literature of the Dominican Republic was written by Spanish religious leaders. The friar Bartolomé de Las Casas wrote a history of the Caribbean, including the Dominican Republic. In his book, he urged the Spanish to act fairly toward the Taínos. Unfortunately, his advice was not taken.

Most Dominican authors write in Spanish, the country's official language. During the 19th century, **unique** styles developed that focused on life in the Dominican Republic. One famous Dominican writer was the poet Pedro Mir, often called Don Pedro. In 1993, he received the Dominican National Prize for Literature. Many people are drawn to his writings, which echo the hopes, dreams, and lives of hardworking Dominicans.

The writer Julia Alvarez, winner of the Pura Belpré Award, was born in New York City, but she was raised mostly in the home country of her Dominican parents. Her books consider the lives of Dominicans and **immigrants**.

A FLAIR FOR FASHION

Dressing neatly, properly, and often formally is especially important in Dominican culture. The long skirts, dresses, and enthusiasm for color that make up traditional Dominican costumes were heavily influenced by Spanish style.

Dominican men frequently wear a shirt called a *chacabana* with long, dark pants. This lightweight shirt is typically white, black, or a light color with hand-sewn decorations. It has two or four pockets on the front and two vertical strips of fabric. The *chacabana* is often worn for special occasions.

Oscar de la Renta is a world-famous fashion designer from the Dominican Republic. His creations have been worn by celebrities around the globe.

Straw hats are a must on this hot and sunny island, whether you are a Dominican or a tourist. Hats with frayed edges are especially popular.

MUSIC AND DANCE

Dominican culture and music are inseparable! The island's streets are filled with the clear beats of merengue, but you will also hear the longing tones of traditional bachata and the intricate sounds of salsa. All three musical styles provide inspiration for dancing, which is a favorite Dominican pastime.

Merengue is the country's most popular music and is played loudly and enthusiastically in many homes and public spaces. The unique sound of merengue developed from European and African influences and traditionally features an accordion, a type of instrument known as a *güira*, and a two-sided drum called a tambora. Merengue is now a couple's dance and is recognizable by its small steps and the dancers' swaying hips. The words of traditional bachata songs tell of romance and life in the country. Couples dance slowly and close together to these emotional songs.

The instrument on the left is the *güira*! Many modern merengue bands combine these three traditional instruments with the strong sound of saxophones.

The *Güira*

Music has a long history in the Dominican Republic. One of the instruments that has survived since the Taíno days is the *güira*. This instrument is used to keep time in merengue and bachata songs. Listen for a rasping sound, and you will have identified the *güira*! The Taíno made theirs out of dried gourds. They kept the rhythm by scraping a stick along the outside of the gourd. Dominicans today have brass *güiras* with metal picks.

SPORTS AND ADVENTURE

The best-loved sport in the Dominican Republic is undoubtedly baseball. In the 1800s, American sailors taught the game to Cubans, who later passed it on to Dominicans. As a nation, they wholeheartedly adopted the sport. There are six professional teams on the island, and many Dominicans also play in U.S. Major League Baseball. These athletes have made Dominicans proud with their record-breaking achievements.

Other popular professional sports in the Dominican Republic include volleyball and boxing. The island's beaches and inviting waters are especially suited for sailing, diving, surfing, kiteboarding, and windsurfing. Hiking provides a healthy way of seeing many stunning mountains, waterfalls, and beaches. Adventurers might even try white-water rafting along the island's longest river, the Río Yaque del Norte.

Baseball star Sammy Sosa is from the Dominican Republic.

Marcos Díaz, the "Dominican Dolphin"

Only one person in the world has connected five different continents by swimming between them. He is Dominican and his name is Marcos Díaz. As a child, Marcos was told he had asthma, so he began swimming to strengthen his lungs. Now a long-distance swimmer, he has crossed the English Channel. He has also swum from New Guinea to Indonesia, from Jordan to Egypt, from Morocco to Spain, and from Russia to Alaska. He once swam twice around Manhattan as a fundraiser for sick children.

DOMINICANS IN AMERICA

  Dominican Americans represent a large portion of the Hispanic population in the United States. Most live in the Northeast, and close to half of all Dominican Americans live in New York City. In the 1960s, Dominicans began to immigrate as a result of political troubles. Since then, the New York City area known as Washington Heights has become home to many Dominican residents. This has resulted in a strong Hispanic community where people can speak Spanish and share their culture together and with others.

  Dominicans have a lot to share with their fellow Americans. Their delicious dishes, fun festivals, moving music, energetic dances, commitment to family and friends, and passion for sports can really strengthen a neighborhood.

Dominican flags are waved along a New York City street for the yearly Dominican Day Parade. Over a million Dominicans live in New York City!

CELEBRATING LIFE

The history of the Dominican Republic is not always easy to study or to understand. Dictators throughout the country's history have encouraged the mistreatment of other people and stood in the way of peace and equality. Yet through all the troubled times, Dominican culture has found a way to thrive and blend the best parts of the country's past into a rich and colorful culture.

The Dominican Republic is truly a mixture of people from different backgrounds. By combining their traditions, they have created new and unique customs. Dominicans know how to celebrate life, with joyful festivals, nature-centered activities, long and tasty meals with family and friends, and the cheerful beat of music keeping time on the island.

GLOSSARY

ancestry: The line of relatives who lived before you.

custom: An action or way of behaving that is traditional among the people in a certain group or place.

dictator: A person who rules a country with total power, often in a cruel way.

elaborate: To have a great deal of detail.

exile: To force someone to leave their home or country.

express: To make something known by showing or telling.

immigrant: A person who comes to a country to live there.

indigenous: Living naturally in a particular region.

interpret: To translate or explain in a new way.

tradition: A way of thinking, behaving, or doing something that's been used by people in a particular society for a long time.

unique: Special or different from anything else.

INDEX

WEBSITES

Due to the changing nature of Internet links, PowerKids Press has developed an online list of websites related to the subject of this book. This site is updated regularly. Please use this link to access the list: www.powerkidslinks.com/chd/domi